Animal Males and Females

For a free color catalog describing Gareth Stevens' list of high-quality books and multimedia programs, call 1-800-542-2595 (USA) or 1-800-461-9120 (Canada). Gareth Stevens Publishing's Fax: (414) 332-3567.

Library of Congress Cataloging-in-Publication Data available upon request from publisher. Fax: (414) 332-3567 for the attention of the Publishing Records Department.

ISBN 0-8368-2712-0

This North American edition first published in 2000 by
Gareth Stevens Publishing
A World Almanac Education Group Company
330 West Olive Street, Suite 100
Milwaukee, WI 53212 USA

This U.S. edition © 2000 by Gareth Stevens, Inc.
First published as *Papa Is Anders Dan Mama* with an original
© 1997 by Mozaïek, an imprint of Uitgeverij Clavis, Hasselt.
Additional end matter © 2000 by Gareth Stevens, Inc.

Text and illustrations: Renne
English translation: Alison Taurel
English text: Dorothy L. Gibbs
Gareth Stevens series editor: Dorothy L. Gibbs
Editorial assistant: Diane Laska-Swanke

Printed in the United States of America

1 2 3 4 5 6 7 8 9 04 03 02 01 00

Animal Males and Females

Renne

Gareth Stevens Publishing
A WORLD ALMANAC EDUCATION GROUP COMPANY

Both of these animals are deer. Although they are the same species, they do not look exactly alike. One is a male deer, and the other is a female deer.

Because they are a male and female of the same species, they can mate someday to have babies. Then the male deer will be a father, and the female deer will be a mother.

buck
(male)

doe
(female)

◄ **4** ►

Here are more males and females of other animal species. Some look alike. Some look different. Male and female animals of the same species often look different. Even if they do not look different, they are different in other ways.

pygmy moths

bearded tits

desert skinks

wrasses

badgers

great diving beetles

hydroids

eagle owls

alpine newts

Why are male and female animals different?

In order to mate, animals must be able to recognize the males and females of their own species.

Many animals recognize each other by how they look — size, color, and features such as antlers or horns. Animals also use other signals to recognize each other, especially scents, sounds, and special kinds of behavior.

These tigers are mammals. Male tigers are usually larger than female tigers, but, other than size, they look almost alike. So, a female tiger makes her presence known by her scent. Tigers recognize each other mostly by scent.

The males and females of these mammal species look different from each other. Features such as shape or color show whether they are male or female.

A female black lemur is rusty brown, but a male is black.

A male lion has a mane, but a female lioness does not.

Male and female whales look the same. The way they look is necessary for living in water, so male and female whales recognize each other by the noises, or sound signals, they make.

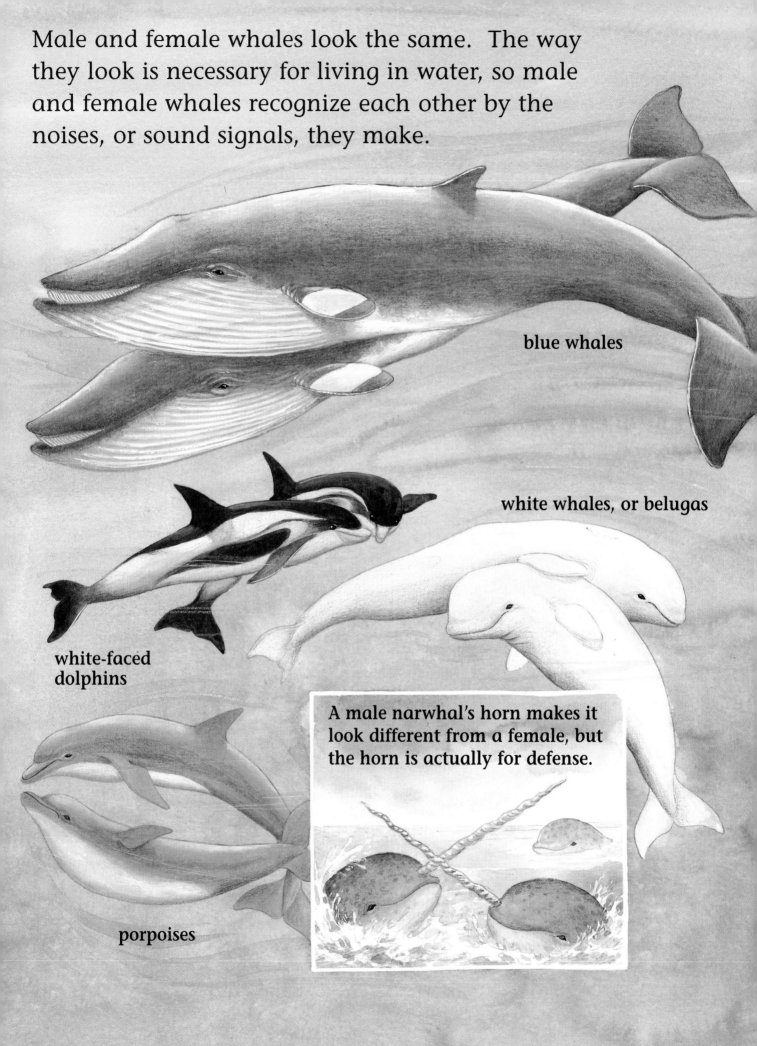

blue whales

white whales, or belugas

white-faced dolphins

A male narwhal's horn makes it look different from a female, but the horn is actually for defense.

porpoises

Elephant seals also use sound signals. The male has a long nose, which he uses like a trunk to make his cry louder. The sound is recognized by both females and other males. It lets everyone know he's around!

cow
(female)

bull
(male)

Some mammals, such as deer, antelope, and gazelles, use more than one signal at a time.

The buck uses a sound signal when he bellows to attract females. At the same time, he shows off his huge antlers.

When a doe sees another deer with antlers, she knows it is a buck. A buck also uses its antlers to impress rival males so they will not attract the females. If it comes to a fight, a male deer will use its antlers as weapons.

A male deer also uses a scent signal, spreading around his strong smell.

Sometimes, a difference between males and females is not always present. In the deer family, for example, males lose their antlers after the mating season.

① spring

② end of spring

⑤ autumn and winter

④ end of summer

③ summer

The antlers grow back before the next mating season.

Marsupial males and females have a very unique difference between them.

young kangaroo in its mother's pouch

koala

Marsupial babies grow in a pouch on their mother's belly. The male does not have a pouch because it does not carry babies.

yellow-footed rock wallabies

wombat

Tasmanian devil

European
Birds

European robin
(female)

gray-headed
woodpecker
(female)

goldeneye duck
(female)

goldeneye
duck
(male)

gray-headed
woodpecker
(male)

merlin
(male)

rock thrush
(male)

European
robin
(male)

Around the world, the biggest difference between male and female birds is how they look. In all of these species, the male birds have brighter coloring than the females.

1. long-tailed minivets
2. gold-winged manakins
3. Vermilion flycatchers
4. blackbirds
5. redstarts
6. collared aracaris

7. Namaqua doves

8. lovely cotingas

9. three-wattled bellbirds

10. eclectus parrots

11. snowy owls

12. regal sunbirds

Male and female birds usually look different. Among these European birds, most of the males are slightly larger than the females of their species. The males of the species also have brightly colored feathers; the feathers of the females are duller colors.

rock thrush
(female)

merlin
(female)

13. great frigate birds
14. Guianian cocks-of-the-rock

peacock
(male)

peahen
(female)

A female bird usually recognizes the male of her species by his beautiful plumage. The brilliant colors and beautiful markings on the male's feathers attract the female for mating.

No two male
ruffs look alike.

pheasant
(male)

ruffs
(male)

pheasant
(female)

ruff
(female)

In most bird species, the male has more brightly colored feathers than the female because, most often, it is the female that hatches the eggs and feeds the young. The female's camouflaged colors help her protect the young by making her less visible in nature.

hummingbirds

A male bird seldom raises its young alone. When it does, however, the male is less brightly colored than the female.

red-necked phalaropes

Male and female birds that look alike must have other ways to recognize each other. A male emperor penguin sometimes takes on a different stance than a female of its species. Penguins also use sound signals.

emperor penguins

Reptiles have very recognizable scents and facial features. The female of a reptile species recognizes a male not only by its size and colors but also by its scent. Sometimes the outer markings on male and female reptiles are different, too.

green lizards

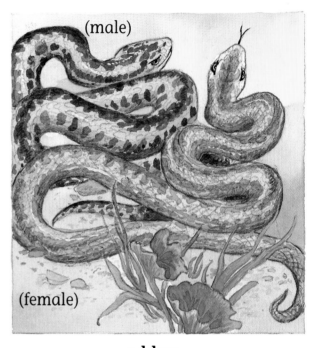
adders

loggerhead turtles

American alligators

Male and female amphibians have their own special signals for mating.

A male water salamander shows off its comb and lively colors to attract a female.

A male frog or toad has an air sac on its throat that makes its calls to females louder.

Because fish can see colors very well, a male fish becomes more colorful, and can even change shape, at the beginning of mating season. These changes attract females.

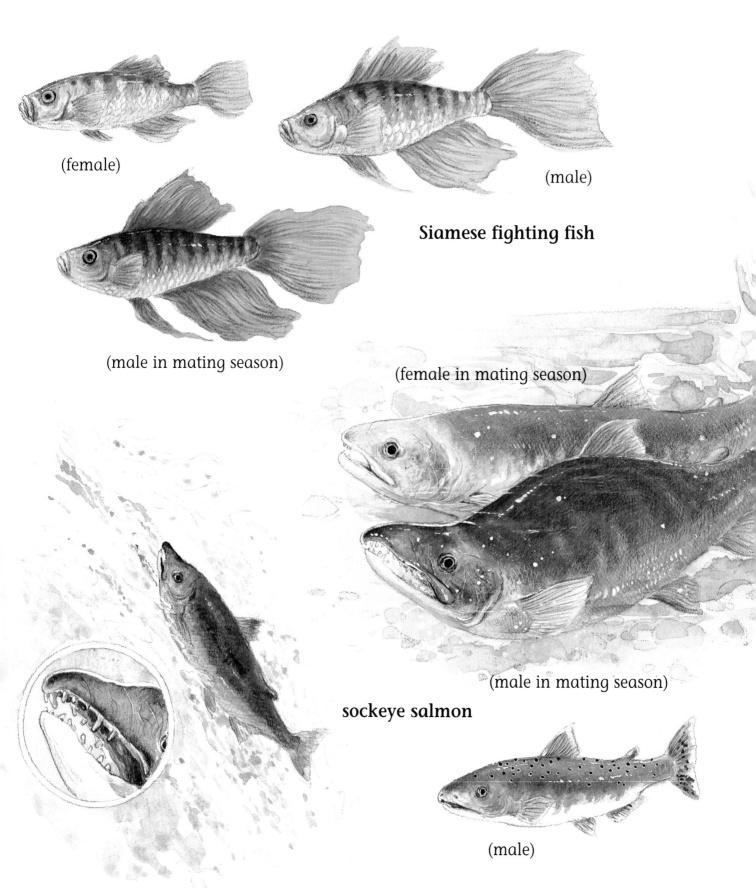

(female)

(male)

Siamese fighting fish

(male in mating season)

(female in mating season)

(male in mating season)

sockeye salmon

(male)

swordtails

(female)

(male in mating season)

(male)

(male)

minnows

(male in mating season)

(female)

three-spined sticklebacks

(male)

(female)

(male in mating season)

(female)

Insects recognize each other mainly by colors and scents. Male insects often have brightly colored markings and larger appendages, such as antennae, than females of their species.

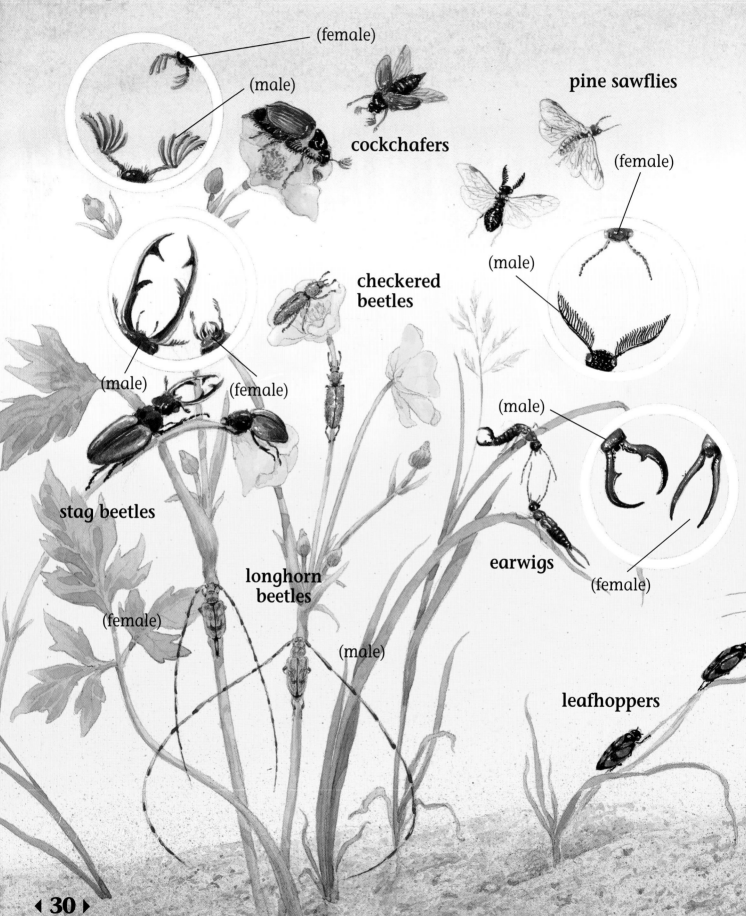

(female)

(male)

cockchafers

pine sawflies

(female)

(male)

checkered beetles

(male)

(female)

(male)

(female)

stag beetles

earwigs

longhorn beetles

(female)

(male)

leafhoppers

When there is no difference at all between the male and female of a species, insects recognize each other by scent.

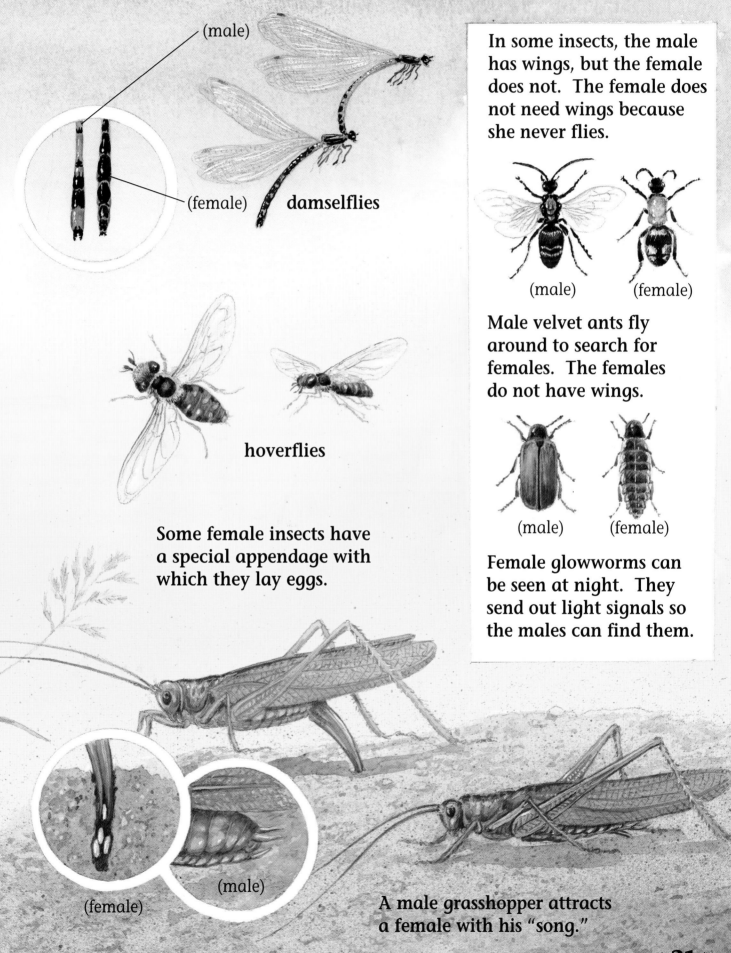

(male)

(female)   damselflies

In some insects, the male has wings, but the female does not. The female does not need wings because she never flies.

(male)   (female)

Male velvet ants fly around to search for females. The females do not have wings.

hoverflies

(male)   (female)

Some female insects have a special appendage with which they lay eggs.

Female glowworms can be seen at night. They send out light signals so the males can find them.

(female)

(male)

A male grasshopper attracts a female with his "song."

Female butterflies that fly during the day are often less colorful than the males of their species. To have a better chance of laying their eggs, the females do not want to attract the attention of predators.

(male)

orange tip butterflies

(female)

Female moths have a scent that attracts the males of their species. Male moths have well-developed antennae so they can catch the scent from far away.

(male)

emperor moths

(female)

Social insects live in unique ways.

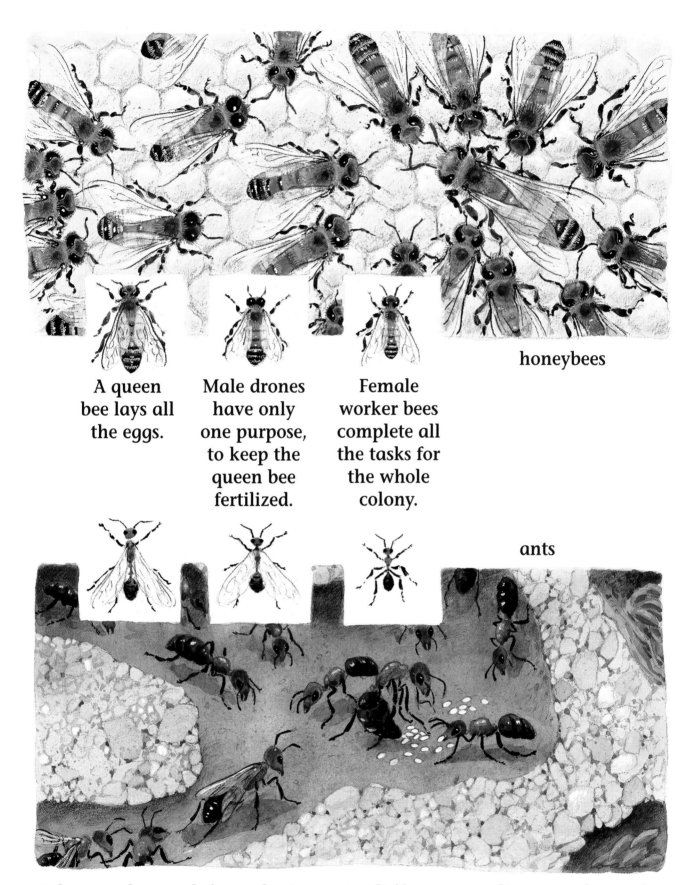

honeybees

A queen bee lays all the eggs.

Male drones have only one purpose, to keep the queen bee fertilized.

Female worker bees complete all the tasks for the whole colony.

ants

The male and female insects differ according to the roles they play in their communities, or colonies.

peacock worms

sea slug

comb jellies

The sea is full of simple creatures. Some of them are both male and female. Most of them do not need each other to produce offspring.

plumose anemones

brittle star

starfish

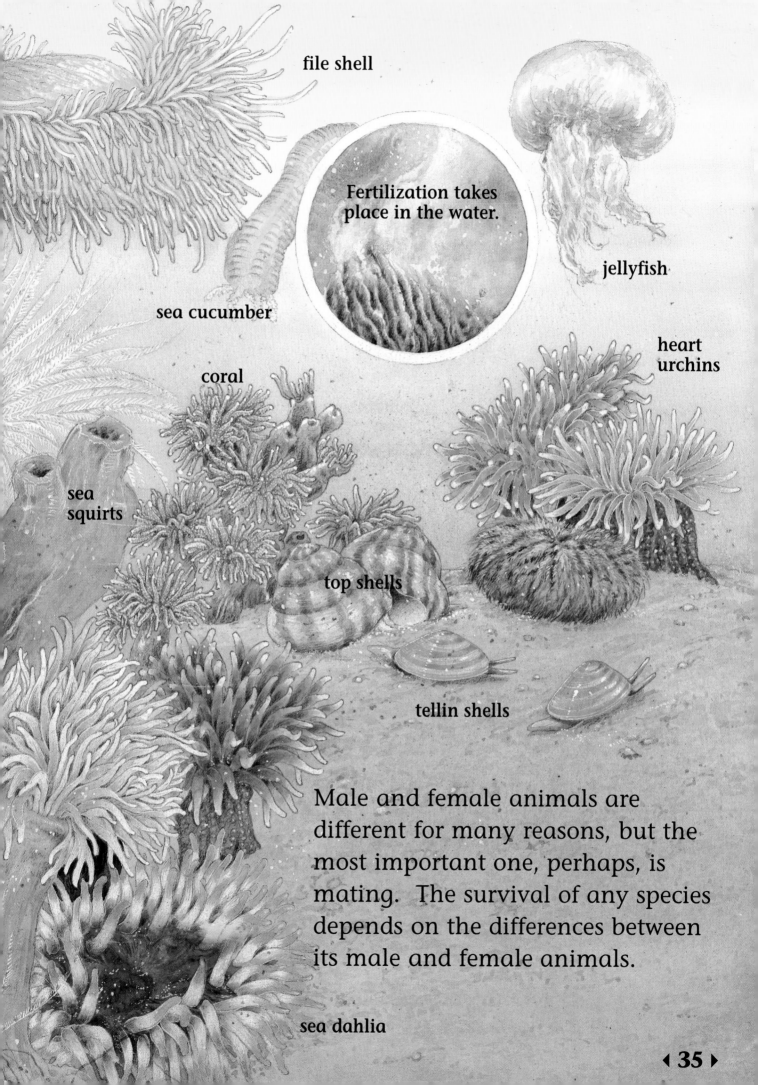

file shell

Fertilization takes place in the water.

jellyfish

sea cucumber

heart urchins

coral

sea squirts

top shells

tellin shells

Male and female animals are different for many reasons, but the most important one, perhaps, is mating. The survival of any species depends on the differences between its male and female animals.

sea dahlia

Glossary

amphibians: animals that are able to live either on land or in the water. A frog is an amphibian. Adult amphibians normally breathe air with lungs, but young amphibians, or larvae, usually have gills and can breathe only in water.

antennae: long, thin sense organs, or "feelers," on the head of an insect. Antennae are often called "feelers" because they are usually used for touching, but some insects use them for smelling, too.

antlers: bonelike appendages on the heads of male mammals such as deer, elk, and moose. Unlike the single-pointed horns on some cattle, sheep, and goats, antlers usually branch out to form many points.

appendages: attachments to something larger; for example, legs, arms, wings, or a tail on the trunk of an animal's body, or antennae on an insect's head.

camouflaged: hidden or disguised, by means of color, shape, or some other feature of appearance, to blend in with the natural surroundings.

colonies: large groups of animals that inhabit defined spaces or areas, living, growing, and working together in an organized and cooperative way.

fertilized: (v) joined together the special male and female cells of an animal species to create the offspring, or young, of that species.

The joined cells usually grow either inside the body of a female animal or inside an egg that is laid by a female animal.

mammals: animals with backbones and hair or fur on their bodies. Female mammals usually give birth to live young and feed them with milk from their bodies.

marsupials: a group of mammals in which females carry their young in a pouch on the outside of their abdomens. Kangaroos and koalas are two well-known marsupials.

mate: (v) to join together for the purpose of producing offspring, or young.

plumage: the covering of feathers on a bird.

predators: animals that hunt and eat other animals.

reptiles: air-breathing animals that have backbones and, usually, slimy or scaly skin. Reptiles move around by sliding on their bellies, like snakes, or crawling on very short legs, like lizards.

scent: the particular smell or odor of an animal or left behind by an animal.

species: a certain group of animals that look and act very much alike and can mate with each other.

stance: a way of standing or positioning the body usually for a specific purpose, such as to send some kind of unspoken message or to display a particular attitude.

More Books to Read

Animal Dazzlers: The Role of Brilliant Colors in Nature. Sneed B. Collard (Franklin Watts)

Animal Fact-File: Head-to-Tail Profiles of Over 90 Mammals. Dr. Tony Hare (Facts on File, Inc.)

Animal Relationships. Animal Survival (series). Michel Barré (Gareth Stevens)

Deer and Elk. Dorothy Hinshaw Patent (Clarion Books)

Making Animal Babies. Sneed B. Collard (Houghton Mifflin)

Partners and Parents. Secrets of the Rainforest (series). Michael Chinery (Crabtree)

Smell. Five Senses of the Animal World (series). Andreu Llamas (Chelsea House)

A Visual Introduction to Whales, Dolphins, and Porpoises. Animal Watch (series). Bernard Stonehouse (Checkmark Books)

What Is a Marsupial? Science of Living Things (series). Bobbie Kalman and Heather Levigne (Crabtree)

Videos

All about Deer. A Video Visit with Jim Arnosky (series). (Library Video)

Animals in Nature (series). (Library Video)

Ants. Bees. Bug City (series). (Schlessinger Media)

Continuing the Line. Trials of Life (series). (Ambrose Video Publishing)

Feathered Friends. Zoo Life with Jack Hanna (series). (Time-Life Video)

Wild Kingdom: New Animal World Collection. (Madacy Entertainment)

Web Sites

Alien Empire: Nature. Welcome to the hive! *www.thirteen.org/nature/ alienempire/multimedia/hive.htm*

Alien Explorers: Birds. *www.alienexplorer.com/ecology/ topic26.html*

NatureExplorer.com. Your Internet Guide to the World of Nature. *www.natureexplorer.com*

SeaWorld/Busch Gardens: Animal Bytes. *www.seaworld.org/ animal_bytes/animal_bytes.html*

To find additional Web sites, use a reliable search engine with one or more of the following keywords: *amphibians, animals, antlers, bees, birds, colors, deer, feathers, fish, insects, mammals, reptiles, seals, smells, sounds, tigers,* and *whales.*

Index